Dearest Margaret & Danielle,

Blessings & thank you for your support. I pray that my poetry books can inspire you both to go after your dreams.

Reconstruction
a book of poetry

Pieces of Life
Volume I

D1708752

Serena Wills

I once dreamt of being published, sharing my writing with the world... and here I am! Never stop striving for your goals!

Much CQ love & blessings,

Published By:
Divine Wryte Creations, LLC

Printed in the United States of America

ISBN-13: 978-1499570298
ISBN-10: 1499570295
Library of Congress Registration Number: TXu 1-695-389

Editing
Dawn Adams
The Training Ground, Inc
Dawn@thetrainingground.us

Cover Art
David Rodriguez
www.drgorilla.com

Author Photo
Dee Hill
www.deehillphotography.com

Cover and Book Design
Stacy Luecker
www.essexgraphix.com

Contributing Artists
Samax Amen
Illustrations
www.ghettomanga.com

Riki Johnson-Atkins
Painter
www.prettyrikiart.com

Soukaa
Queen of Sorrow
Soukaa@aol.com

Adinkra Symbols and Definitions taken from the Adinkra Dictionary by W. Bruce Willis

Dedication

This book is dedicated to my Iya (mother)
Marguerite "Sauti" Wills.
May 20, 1949-February 19, 2010
Thank you for always encouraging me.
My Nana, Bernice Wills who is blessed to see 90 years of life.
My son Jordan Oladele Ince.
I couldn't imagine life without you.
A blessing sent from God with a divine purpose. I love you.

ODO NNYEW FIE KWAN

"Love never loses its way home"
Adinkra symbol of the power of love
(Willis, The Adinkra Dictionary)

ACKNOWLEDGMENTS

The birth of my first poetry book couldn't be possible without the blessings of my Father God. I was lost for a little while, and ready to give up. But between prayer and knowing that God was bringing me out of my storms, trials and tribulations I learned how to live again. Battling a chronic illness was hard but I kept my faith and believed that I would be totally healed and restored from Lyme Disease. I'm thankful to my heavenly Father for divine healing.

Mom, (my Iya Marguerite "Sauti" Wills), life wouldn't have been the same without your continuous love, encouragement, motivation, inspiration and the fight to move forward. Mom was what I called a silent fighter. She didn't make a lot of noise or raucous, but she taught me that you can fight for what you believe in and not make a show or production out of it. Her name, Sauti means voice because she spoke nothing but knowledge and power. Thank you Mom for your gifts and love.

My wonderful grandparents, Mrs. Bernice Wills and the late Lawrence Wills Sr., you helped Mom raise me. It was a joy growing up with all of you. You embraced my imagination and encouraged me at a young age to write about our adventures.

God blessed me with my son Jordan Oladele Ince in 2011. I can't imagine how life would be without you Jordan. Thank you for giving me joy every day and I know God and the ancestors will protect you as you grow and develop. The future has so much in store for us.

My sisters Shavonn Hayes, the late Ayana Wills and Christina Wills. I don't know what I would have done without your love. Although Ayana is gone, we have kept her memory alive and her spirit has a way of circling around all of us. Shavonn, we didn't get to know each other until I was 25 and you were 19 because of the missing pieces in our family. But I feel as though we grew up together. I love you so much. Christina, my diamond in the rough, I love to hear you sing in the mornings when I'm visiting home. Even though your biological mother made a mistake of becoming addicted to crack through her mistakes we were blessed with the gift of your life. I'm so happy Mommy adopted and nurtured you.

I have sisters that aren't blood but I believe God put them into my life for a divine reason and we are truly family. I love each of you for being in my life for months to years! I had a few sisters that nursed me back to health. I know Mom sent an angel to be by my side physically when she sent Janice into my life. I was almost bed-ridden at one point and she swooped into my life and I can never say enough about how much she cared for me. Mommy sent her and I will always be eternally grateful for her love!

I have so many sista girls…too many to name but all of you know that you're loved and I thank you all for being in my corner during the great times and through the storms.

To all of my beautiful godchildren, nephews and children in my life, Kayla, Angel and Daquaan (DJ), Rahiem (can't wait to see you in the NFL draft in the future), Kuwon and Zaire, Nicholas, Dontae, Noah and Noemi, Jazz and Zane, Justin and Ryan, Tyler and Bryce, Isaiah, Norman, Marley, Domonique and Elijah, Bailey, Jay, Ryan, Sophia, Jaxon and Amani.

I have to acknowledge the host of family on all sides, Wills, Douglas and Hayes and my extended family. I truly love you. Also I have to give a shout out to those beautiful Sorors of mine of Delta Sigma Theta Sorority Inc.

My father figures and brothers who've given me confidence and advice when I didn't want to hear it and encouragement. I love each of you for stepping in and embracing me. Praise God for the father figures. All of you are awesome and I love each of you.

All of my Virginia Tech and Syracuse University family, Central Park East Secondary School and CPE 1, I say thank you and to the teachers (Santiago, Cosbie, Shirley, Pat, Jeremy, Bruce, David and Steve Fiekes (my writing consultant at SU) that would rip my writing apart only to make me piece it back together. Now I know why you did what you did and I'm extremely thankful for the hard edits back then and the encouragement you gave me.

Thank you to my family of The International Afrikan American Ballet. A dynamic African dance company from the 70s through the 80s. You watched me grow from a baby into the woman that I am now. Thank you for embracing me after my sweet mother departed to heaven in 2010. Your love and constant nurturing means a lot to me and my family. Many blessings to all of you and may we always stay connected!

Special thanks to my editor Dawn Adams of The Training Ground and readers Erica Davis, Candace Givens, David Herman and Darius Frasure and Venetta Pittman. I would like to thank my graphic designer Stacy Luecker of Essex Graphix for the book cover layout, interior typeseting and her creative skills and friendship. You can find her at www.essexgraphix.com. The design artist for my cover, David Rodriguez, who is a gifted painter and the piece you see is titled "Trust" check him out at www.drgorilla.com, and illustrator Samax Amen, for the pieces you'll see throughout the book. Check out more of his illustrations and support his business at www. ziontific.com and www.ghettomanga.com, as well as painter Soukaa (creator of Queen of Sorrow). For more information on Soukaa's work please email her at soukaa@aol.com I would also like to thank Riki Johnson-Atkins, painter, as she contributed multiple pieces to the book. You can see more of her art throughout the Dallas/Fort Worth area at shows and galleries. Her website is www.prettyrikiart. com and she can also be contacted by email at prettyrikiart@gmail. com. The beautiful author's photo was taken by a dear friend of mine that has the gift of photography, Ms. Dee Hill. Her website is www. deehillphotography.com. Also thank you to Renee Johnston who created and maintains my website. You can visit her site at http://www. nazick.com.

Dedicated to the wonderful arts collectives, organizations and writers groups that have given me steam when I ran out, embraced all of my creativity "and not pieces of it" and encouraged me; Art Conspiracy, ArtLoveMagic, The Writers Block, South Dallas Cultural

Center (thanks Mama Vicki, Tisha and Harold), Guerilla Arts Ink, Sojournals, Liberated Muse, Preservation LINK and Journey Man Ink.

The spiritual guidance of my church homes Ebenezer AME in Ft. Washington, MD and Oak Cliff Bible Fellowship in Dallas, TX.

To all of my friends, poets, writers, authors, artists, communities that I've served, keep striving. I know times are tough but we will all come out on top! Thank you for loving me, mentoring and being an inspiration to me. To the ones that are near to my heart you know who you are and I love you. Blessings to all of my friends and those battling and healing from chronic illnesses; just know I'm in the fight with each of you. Praying for our daily healing and total restoration. Becoming sick made me realize so much that I wanted to do. I used to "think" about doing something...now I just do it. Life is so precious and all of those who fight the battle of illnesses whether its Lyme Disease, Lupus, Chrone's Disease, AIDS, Cancer...etc...I pray that when we are out of the woods that we are even stronger and better than ever! That's my prayer for each of you whether I know you or not.

Praises to the medical team of The Institute for Multidimensional Medicine (TIMM). Dr. Sakiliba Mines and her staff embraced me from the moment I dragged myself into her clinic and she promised me that she would be by my side to get me back to full health. I learned so much about the power of integrative medicine but most importantly I found out that there are doctors and practices like hers that care about each of their patients. May God continue to rain His blessings down on you Dr. Mines and your staff. I would like to thank the rest of medical/holistic team, I love you all.

Lastly to all of my ancestors that have passed on, as we say in the African tradition, Ase, Ase, Ase.

Peace and Love,
Serena T. Wills

INTRODUCTION

The series of poems you're about to read, comes from various pieces of situations that I have experienced in my life. We've all been in love, heartbroken, enraged, complacent, depressed, wondered if we were to blame for everything that's gone wrong. I prayed through rough times not understanding what was going on, the "why me" phase was in full effect. I had no idea that I was being built up through my trials and tribulations, so that one day I could overcome the battle. I'm a strong believer in prayer and I know that through it, my work and servant-hood, I would get through the storms no matter how short or long they may be.

You might be in the middle of a storm or just beginning of one. Some of you may not see it on the horizon; you think everything is perfect like a sunny day. You're ignoring the signs that something may be brewing, you're in denial. A few of you have gone through the storms and picked this book up to remind you of the reconstruction that you went through and how you were taken apart and put back together.

All or some poems will hit home for you whether you have been in love, or found the one person that is your soul mate or you're carrying your husband's child. You might be going through the maze called transition when everything has gone haywire to say the least and you see the clouds forming when the one you love no longer wants you. You may feel mentally trapped and blame yourself wondering, did you do something to cause the train wreck. You've gone through the transition and now feel the fiery aftermath of rage and fury. Hoping that you won't let the darkness overtake your life to the point of hurting someone or even yourself.

One day at the end of your travels, through the valley that was once full of good ole lovin' which turned into mass deconstruction, you can see the horizon. The sun is beginning to peek through the storm clouds as you ask for restoration and begin the process of reconstruction.

Whether it's a silent prayer, meditation, or whatever you positively do to cleanse your spirit, it begins to take place. I reminisced on my journey to Africa during a difficult period of my life. I recalled how that excursion was life changing. By experiencing different cultures, learning Zulu, touching the Indian Ocean, constant prayer and writing I learned forgiveness. Life is too short to dwell on the past. We have to be like Sankofa, "Learn from it to build for the future."

Life isn't perfect and we all have our journey; but your knowledge on this trip through the valley could help someone else who is going through the storms. I invite you to read my journey of poetry titled, "Reconstruction, Pieces of Life, Volume 1." Enjoy, learn, cry, meditate, and lose yourself for a moment in these pieces. Listen to what your heart and spirit are telling you. Use the blank pages throughout the book to write your own thoughts and reflections. Just write as a dear friend and spoken word artist once told me, "Poetry is to be received and not judged." So go for it, the sky's the limit.

Let go of yesterday
to live for today
to build for tomorrow.

God bless and thank you for supporting my endeavors.

TABLE OF CONTENTS

ACT IV - Reconstruction

Reconstruction
a book of poetry

Act I

Good Ole Lovin'

I WAS SOOOOOO IN LOVE...

He loved me

In a special way

And I in return

Loved him too

Nothing could go wrong

I loved him

Unconditionally

Like no other would

Or could

There is nothing like

That old fashion

Love making by day or night

Anywhere in sight

Kind of love

Good Ole Lovin'

FIERY TRESSES
BY Riki Johnson-Atkins

BREATHTAKING

Looking into your eyes

I see the sun rise

As it spreads through the valley

When I touch you

I feel the warmth of the Sahara Desert

And the comfort of a cool wind

On a hot summer day

Loving you is *easy* and satisfying to my soul

Being with you brings a sensation to my spirit
that I've never felt before

It feels as if the ancestors embraced me,
held my hand and God directed me to you

My prayer to God was to bless me with my King

And here you stand before me

As you touch my face with your gentle hand I
feel a vibe I've never felt before

Kisses are breathtaking

Whisking me away, making me forget my prob-
lems, fears and my hurtful past

Lying beside you, kissing you, touching you
and loving you; I've been yearning
for a love like this since the beginning of time

Time stands still when I'm with you,
as we make sweet memories together

Looking into your eyes,
I see the gentle waves of the Indian Ocean

Touching you, I feel that warm sensation
that will never go away

Loving you is so right

Feeling you like this is so real

Being your woman is a joy

Soul mates we are...now...and forever

FREEDOM SUNSET
BY Riki Johnson-Atkins

SWEET LOVE JONES

I gotta a love jones

It jumped into my soul

I don't know how to explain it

Or how I've even obtained it

It's a feeling only one would know

When they're in love

This feeling has made its way through my bones
that I can only show him

Beginning to wonder and search for answers as
to why I feel electric within

When we are intertwining and unwinding

Emotions jet out like a racing stream
right before the waterfall

There's no control over these emotions that
flood my spirit

As my man whispers in my ear

My body melts and my soul is awakened
by the sound of his voice

His tender but hard strokes make me know
how much he loves me

When a man can stroke your intelligence

Feed your spirit and physically connect

What more could you want from this King

I watch him sleeping

Knowing that

I'm dancing through his dreams

As we lay underneath the sun rising

Listening to the sweet birds chirping

I thank God for yet another day

Nothing like a sweet love jones

Overtaking our souls

Loving each other forever more

HEARTS ON FIRE
BY Riki Johnson-Atkins

GRAVITY

Your energy pulls me to a place
and lifestyle I have never seen

It's been a long time since
I've been stroked mentally

Most brothers just want it physically

No not you, you are different

You'd rather intertwine in my mind

Instead of giving me some sorry line

You are cut from a different piece of cloth

One that I've never seen, felt or touched

It's as soft as lamb's wool

But it's as tough as leather

Valuing friendship is much deeper
than having a physical escapade

This is why I'm digging you

It's almost as if you are setting the stage
for one of your shows

Wanting everything right

All you need now is your mic

So I can hear your raspy voice better

Your words are striking

Presence is tempting

Hugs are fulfilling

Kisses like chocolate

I too want to get to know you

Willing to sacrifice the physical

Wanting the spiritual and mental

Our aura and energy together
is something for everyone to see

We should embrace the possibilities
of this beautiful friendship and attraction

I have yet to show you

How my friend, my man will be in my life

And how our friendship will never
unravel or be broken

We are one source of energy, a surge of light

That no human can control

It's the best feeling to have a friend that looks at
you in every light

Who loves you for you

A companion that is straight up feeling you

Blowing one's mind

In time, hoping that gravity will keep pulling us
to a place that I can only dream of with you

EPIPHANY

Lovemaking to my soul

Reaching down into places

Where no one should go

But somehow you're there with the power

Of your voice, singing blues and your guitar

Strumming the chords of my creative muse

Musical depth of the ocean's floor

Longing for a moment with you

Visualization of musically twisted thoughts

Poetry with your grooves

Rhythm and blues

Reggae to even country tunes

Tapping into me

Like the army uses Morse code

Asking myself, "How do you know what to touch,
press, feel and even stroke...creatively"

Longtime coming since I let go into this abyss
of my natural mystic

Tucked away, never wanting to get hurt

Guarded from the fear

Of the past troubles

One man tried to rape my artistry, creativity and mentality

He didn't believe in the power of music

Words bouncing off of the walls

Bass trembling to the bottom of my toes

To the tips of my eyelashes

Discovery once again, through you,
my musical incline

An epiphany wondering
what was missing from my life

Uniquely designed as I come alive again

Loving you

Digging you

Plugging away at those guitar strings

Wanting you as you sing to me
through your soft lips

Rejuvenation of my mind, body and spirit

Creative restoration

God placed this gift in you

Blessing others with your tunes

Swaying to the music…nothing but the music

Lovingly through you

ONE BEAT GOODNIGHT

Dancing the night away

Bumping and grinding as the beats play

Gazing into each other's eyes

Staring deeper you get hypnotized

By the strong vibe that he is sending

When he pulls you closer

Caressing your back, arms and thighs

Topping it off, he decides to lie

Passionate kisses upon your lips

As you think to yourself, "
He is it...the man God blessed me with"

You can't help but to wonder

What lies beneath and under

This mysterious man's exterior

When he touched your hand,
you knew he was the man

Rocking back and forth to a slow jam

Then the night was coming to an end

When you went to walk away

He grabbed your waist and whispered, "Please
stay

We cannot end our night like this,
without one more long sweet kiss."

Finding yourself kissing this man

Taking your hand

He leads you into a room filled with darkness

Candles lit, laying you down and starts to un-
dress

Journey beginning to tranquility

Embracing each other tight

His touches are with tenderness

He kisses you softly, with his lips

Escaping to paradise, into bliss

Dawn begins to arise

Rolling over to think about this man

Who has stolen your heart

At times it's hard to believe that he is your man,
lover and friend

Drifting off comforted by sleep

With thoughts that this love will last
until the end of time

MOONLIT PATH

Light shining through my window
in the dark of night

Sitting in deep thought

Watching the clouds move
until they covered the moon

Scented candles and incense burning
so their sweet aromas float through the air

I hear you rummaging through the house
after a hard day at work

Hoping you would be attracted to the smell

My heart skips a beat
as I hear you climb the steps

I think back to when we met in the park,
it feels like yesterday

The warm breeze blew through my hair
and the leaves twirled around
as you approached me in the still of the night

Music was playing, people were talking
and a man was juggling for money

The path was lit by the rays of the moon
as we moved in closer to one another

All I could see was you

When I gazed into your eyes I felt at peace

That moment told me that you were the one

We sat on a bench nearby and talked for hours

The sound of your voice softened my soul
and made me warm inside

The midnight hour approached

We walked down the street
and held hands like old friends

We stood at the foot of my stoop and faced one another

You softly pressed your lips on mine

Chills went down my spine when you ran
your fingers through my hair and massaged my scalp

The night finally ended
with one last passionate kiss as you walked away

That kiss has been on my lips ever since

I look at you now even more
in love than the day we met

Finally you enter the doorway to our bedroom, after
much anticipation

Strong hands began to massage the small of my back

Body shivering and my toes
are tingling at your every touch

You take my hand and turn me around

Making your way down as you begin to rub my pregnant
belly that is holding our first born

Lying in your arms as we drifted off to sleep,
the warm breeze from the window
drifts through the room

It takes me back to the night we met
on the moonlit path

Where our roads crossed will forever be in my soul

The rays of the moon showered down on us

It was the moonlit path that led me to you

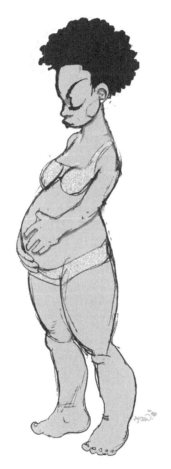

MOTHER TO BE
BY Samax Amen

JOURNAL NOTES

JOURNAL NOTES

JOURNAL NOTES

ACT II

Transitional Issues

THEN CAME THE STORM...

People trip

No not my soul mate

How would he...

How could he

Trip on me so deeply

I slipped up

Putting too much of me

Into him

Broken into pieces

In a snap

Transition at its worst

QUEEN OF SORROW
BY Soukaa

DARK CLOUDS ON A BLUE DAY

As tears stream down my face

Sitting here trying to erase thoughts of the past

I wish would have never happened

The day finally coming to an end

I know couples have their days

The ones that they wish would never phase

Their relationship that is strong

It seems as if nothing could go wrong

Until that day appears

Then we fear

What becomes of it

Hoping that the cause is just a tiff

I say this because it can be overlooked

Or evenly simply mistook

Especially when it's your first outburst

You have together

Something that can be taken as light as a feather

BUT IT CHANGES ABRUPTLY
LIKE THE WEATHER

Going through the motions

Like a sailboat out on the rocky ocean

Then it hits the fan

Like an earthquake shaking the land

You know that something is definitely wrong

You fuss, fight and cry

Heart feels like it died

And then before you know it

The simple tiff

Is lit like a stick of dynamite

It ignites

You cry

Staring into outer space

Wondering where

All this tension came from

Heart palpitating like a drum

Suddenly it ends

The day once so damn blue

If only he knew

How hurt you are

One night left a scar

You wonder where those dark clouds rolled in from

Mentally browsing

Through the day that was once blue

But now…it's finally through

UNCONDITIONAL

Loving your man can be such a joy

A pleasantry to say the least

If he knew that your heart stops when you see him

Thinking to yourself, "He's breathtaking."

If he knew how much
you appreciated his will and effort

If only he knew
the unconditional love that you have for him

Love that is so real
that you can't see yourself without him

But you feel that he chooses to not see it

Everyone has their ups and downs

Despite his blindness
you still love him unconditionally

Rewind to the other day when he told you,

"You Make Me Sick!"

Shaking your head as you thumped your hands
on his chest screaming, "Stop It!"

He doesn't care about your needs and desires

How draining your job is taking notes
for someone who doesn't care about your future

Coming home to a man
who doesn't appreciate your efforts

It's enough to drive you straight crazy!!!!

Even though your love continues to be unconditional

Hurting at night you cry yourself to sleep
and weep to God for the madness to cease

Hurtful words sink deep into the open wounds
of your soul from the last argument

Although you are honest with him,
respect trust, and show passion for him

The words echo in your head
from past arguments

Over some pettiness

Screaming internally,
*"LOVE ME FOR EVERYTHING THAT I AM
AND NOT PIECES OF ME!"*

You finally realize no man is
or ever will be perfect

Yet, you can't stop loving him

Even though what he bestows

Are blows to your spirit

Praying for all the wrong things

Maybe God doesn't want you with him
but you keep loving him

Sad part is...

He
Doesn't
Love you
Anymore

BURNING BURDEN

A burden on my soul

So heavy that I don't know how to shake it

Or how to break it

Reminiscing on those I've lost

Jobs that are gone

The piece of spirit that is done

All I can ask is, "What went wrong?"

Why was my Daddy snatched away from me
before I knew him?

And what about Papa, Sister Ayana,
Aunt June and Uncle Freddy?

I miss them so much and wish they were around

Missing someone is a strain on the heart

Never knowing when or even if the pain will go away

There's a burden on my soul

Don't know how to pay the bills
or where the next penny lays

How can I make my dreams come true?

At my ripe age I feel tired and worn

Tired of the pain that I'm going through
just to make a living

Spirit and soul are weary and need rejuvenation

Soul needs love and adornment

It wants to be nurtured and know
that everything is going to be alright

Right now I don't feel that

Trying to be this perfect woman that I'm not

Missing the old me that was so carefree
and put myself first...where did I go?

Feeling lost, praying
for something good to come my way

Praying for happiness

Peace...

Solutions...

May God have mercy on me
through my path and pain, as He comforts me

EVERYDAY TRIPPIN'

Trippin'

Everyday, every week there's always sumthin'

People's minds are so focused on them that they
don't even know when they are buggin'

Trippin'

It's the holiday season and although
I give thanks I am steadily mournin'

Over the death of my sister, my friend,
my spiritual partner

I am trying as I pray to God
to keep my mind from buggin'

But it's hard to stay focused and light
when there is always someone trippin'

Always over sumthin'

People get offended over the slightest mess

When their minds are not looking
at the bigger picture

Simple miscommunication
takes folks to another dimension

Wires get crossed and even though I say
I am sorry they're constantly taking

A trip...as they slip...and bug out
into another world

I am trying Lord,
I am trying to not lose my mind

As peeps constantly trip, every day, every week;
it's always sumthin

If I stay to myself then why is it a question

Can this sista get her thoughts in order
and focus on the one man that I know
won't let me down

My God, my Savior as He never lets me fall...
down into a pit so deep that I can't climb out

See peeps are buggin', trippin' and slippin'
every day of the week and I am not going

There with you as I am trying to survive
this holiday season

Whether you are family or friend, just know...

That I will never let you take me down
and I'm not in the mood to clown around

As I said before and I'll say it again,
I'm tryin' to get through this period of mournin'

But as my good God lets me know
I am not the one trippin' and He will bless those
who are steadily mournin'

So pack your baggage, take your trip
and let me be...if you can't understand
I am not the one to trip out
on every day of the week and no I don't want it
to always be sumthin'...

BLING DREAMS

He was a crack fiend

Dope fiend

Smoking that pipe

Called the American dream

He went from rags to riches

Thinking of cars, clothes and materialistic items

Pipe dreaming, smoking that crack pipe
full of money, jewels and women

That couldn't care for him

Or even dare to look out for a brother

Loving money, rims and blinged cuff links

As you just walk around dumbfounded

The life you once envisioned

Has been clouded with your selfish schemes

As you fulfilled your pipedreams

You thought you went from ashy to classy

Except the women weren't calling you
Big Poppa

Nope, not those who only saw the money
and your cover up that you want to call life

As you battle with your internal demons

Dissing friends who've been
in your corner forever

Forgetting about the times
you were admitted to the hospital

The time you didn't have a dime
and we got you out of trouble

We no longer fit into your bracket

That wannabe income level
that you steadily wave in our faces

And it's cool...just look to us
when those demons come after you again

And again

And again

Keep smoking that crack pipe full of Blackberrys
or what I call Crackberrys,
wannabe important meetings,
driving in a blinged out car
while you still live with your parents

Check yourself before someone else does

I was once your Queen

The one you shared your dreams and goals with

Half on a baby and the house with the backyard

But you tried to crush me
as you made that move on up the corporate ladder

Stopped taking those meds to even yourself out

Or was it the time you
decided to move on up into the deluxe loft

With that jacked up credit report

You were high on yourself

Smelling yourself

And forgetting about all those
who were in your corner

You forgot about me...

But this is my goodbye letter to you

Cause I am happier without ya

My dreams are real and my passions
are being fulfilled

This is what we call life my brother

Realizing that I made a mistake

Instead of allowing Him
to lead a man to me

I lead myself to you

Our paths unwound rapidly

As you are steadily

Smoking the crack pipe
called material things

Trying to live in a bling dream

What you think is the American way

I'm letting the anger go...

You took too much of my time
and it is time to let it go...

Just wake up brother

Wake up

Before you lose more

JOURNAL NOTES

JOURNAL NOTES

JOURNAL NOTES

Act III

Aftermath

AND I NEVER SAW IT COMING...

Darkness in my life

Changes made mid season

Aftermath of what I just learned

Trying to keep my head above water

In the floods

As I sink into depression

Trying to stay afloat

Praying

I won't kill you first

Welcome to the aftermath

ADDICTS MOAN

Like a flower in the darkness

Wilting away in sadness

Wishing it would all come to an end

Not knowing what will happen

As the seconds tick
and I notice time fading away

I feel limp, I can't move

My roots are dry

Becoming weak

When will the pain go away?

I fall deeper

Soaking up everything negative

Do I love myself?

Can I be me again?

Wondering what happened

As he stole my soul and left me to die

Given up hope

As my leaves begin to fall off

Petals turn into a shade of grey

Please stop!!!!!

Take the pain away; I just want it to end

Come on just give me one hit

What do I have to do to feel again?

Selling my soul to the devil, I'll pay the price

Don't you understand?

All I wanted to do was feel good
and float on cloud nine

Hit after hit has destroyed me

No home to live in, not a damn dime in the bank

My family has abandoned me

Looking deeper into myself

I'm dried up like a wilted flower

My petals have fallen

Just one hit, c'mon...
one last hit to make the pain end

BROKEN

Words cannot replace one's presence

It can't replace their style, kiss or essence

Words make you aware
of what you think they feel

But what about those who are affectionate
and want pure lovin'

So how can one get your attention

When your loved one lies next to you
in the dark of night

And whispers, "Baby don't worry, I still
love you, my feelings haven't changed for you"

I wish I could believe you

But you are out most nights

Walking in with the morning

When I need you

You are nowhere to be found

Simply out of sight

Yet I still love you

I want to stop feeling broken

You have said things
and never followed through

Put a ring on my finger expecting me to say I Do

I used to be your lucky star

But I have come face to face with a brick wall

Our relationship

Is not there anymore

Yet I still try to smile

Yearning for your love

Hoping to break down the barrier between us

MENTAL BONDAGE

Mind is trapped

By this demon

He has wrapped his arms around my mentality

And has my spirit in bondage

I chose to give in 'cause I was tired of fighting

Too many meds and no sleep was getting tiring

Tired of waiting for God to work miracles

So I trusted myself and fixed myself...I think

I got demons in my system
and I don't know how to shake 'em

Friends and loved ones, kept trying to tell me what to do

When to do

How to do

Too many doctors to count

Just testing me out

So I stopped doing everything
that was supposed to help me

And now the person in front of you
is one that I don't even know

I am somebody else...and I keep losing people around me

Just can't get around the meds

Physiological insanity that constantly brews

From childhood to manhood, countless battles I lose

Even questioning my faith

Not knowing what to do

Why do I have to live
with demons inside my soul

Why do I lock God out
when others tell me He is in control

Continuing to lose people,
jumping from woman to woman

Man to man who I think are my soul mates

So maybe one day I will let God in

In the meantime
I guess I have to become friends

With the demons that live within

I know I have a choice to make

But I feel so weak

Vulnerable

At times I feel evil

So pray for me and maybe one day

I will let the Lord into my life

Let Him fight off these demons
that have a hold on my mentality

This thing called life

DAY DREAMER
BY Samax Amen

TRADING YOU IN

He no longer desires me

Hair too thick

Curves too much

And the complexion of my skin

Just not light enough

The man I once knew

Faded away

Throughout the years

I saw him stray away

He wasn't true to himself

So how could he be to me

Hanging with the homies

Trying to blend in

When behind closed doors

He was creeping

And as much as I tried to comply
with his every need

I lost him

He traded in my curves

The kinkiness of my hair

He hated my dark brown eyes

Instead of a strong woman
Traded me in for a yes girl

Brother caught up between two worlds

Saying "Yes sir, no sir" by day

And "what up" to the homies at night

He sold himself short

Turned into something else

Before my very eyes

Didn't understand that he could not
balance both worlds

Just gotta be true to yourself first

Trying to pimp and profile
like he is living the glamorous life

Keeping up with the Jones' instead of himself

Going for broke to impress his new delight

He sold himself out
saying one thing to one world

Switching up the lingo for the new girl

Pray for the man 'cause he's lost

Looking for acceptance in the wrong place

He is not He anymore

Traded in his soul

His friends

His girl

Then he played around

Trading in his faith

DEAR LOVE

Dear Love

I thought I knew you

Once adored your every move

Your style and grace

How is it that the thing I love

Could be so hurtful

The kind of love I thought I had

Was something that I envisioned
to be untouchable

Approachable and something like no other

Again I failed at love,
at what I thought it was supposed to be

Wondering if one day I will find that one

That will love me for who I am,
my spirit and everything

He will look past my flaws
and love me for my inner beauty

It will be that old fashion, old school love

Never have to guess or have a second thought

It will be plain as day and the pursuit will be hot

But alas I don't know if I will ever find that love

Or if that love will ever find me

Scared that I will grow old

Not knowing what that will ever feel like
with a man

Fear that there is no one out there for me

Times are hard God and I am trying

Keep my faith knowing that one day
you will bless me with my mate

But today I am in a dark place

Not knowing how to face

The man I thought was the one

Now I know God that I jumped the gun

Tired of my feelings being trampled on

Anger building up inside me

As the days go on and I grow older

Wondering if there is one

Praying for patience and a light heart
But it's hard God

It's hard because I thought I knew
who you blessed me with

But in return

His eye is on someone else

And yes, again I have to face the fact that,
I was wrong

So God please shed light on me

Cause I am in a dark place tonight

BEFORE I LET GO
BY Samax Amen

LOST

Lord I miss him

No explanation

Or any connotation

Why I love him

Years of battles

Struggle, Hurdles and Fear

Friendship come and gone

But yet

I yearn for him

The devil intervened

In our love

This man took my heart

To places that no one will ever know

Understanding

Me

Accepting

Me

For all that I could give

But yet

The devil intervened

On my journey

To what was called love

What can I do

Please help me heal

Understand that all this suffering

Anxiety

Insecurity

Will lead me to a place

Where I won't feel lost

The journey with him is over

Done

No longer friends

Help me get to a place

No hurt

Or unfulfilled promises

An escape

From my feelings

Help me to understand

That he was a person

Meant for a reason

And only one season

In my life

JOURNAL NOTES

JOURNAL NOTES

JOURNAL NOTES

JOURNAL NOTES

Act IV

Reconstruction

SALVATION
BY Riki Johnson-Atkins

THEN IT WAS TIME
TO TAKE LIFE BACK...

Overcoming my demons

Climbing mountains

In this thing called life

No longer

Feeling defeated

Depleted

I redirected my energy

Into my love

Writing

Therapy for the soul

Cleansing as I traveled to places

Only people imagine

Blessings began to flow

I've won the battle

During this time

Of reconstruction

DROPS OF AGAPE
BY Riki Johnson-Atkins

SOUNDS OF THE OCEAN

Listen...she said...Stand still...
close your eyes and listen to what they say

Our ancestors are here
and their spirits are beside me

Guiding me to the Indian Ocean

As I stand at the shore,
I kneel down in the wet sand and pray

Giving many thanks to those who walked before
me

Those who have shown me
and who are physically with me

Reflecting on my ancestors who were once en-
slaved and taken from their Motherland

They make the world go round as they talk to
me through the crashing waves

"Just listen," my friend said
as she grabs my hand

Inhaling the fresh air focusing
on the lay of the land

Disbelief that I'm standing in South Africa

In the background I hear the children's laughter
and the wind talking

Season changing before me

Reminiscing on moments in time
with a deep sigh of relief

Realizing that everything,
good and bad, happened for a reason

Praising His name because I am here and alive

Here we stand on the coast of Durban
Once again just listen...shhhhh...

God is here...give thanks

For He has made my paths straight

Communicating to me today
Through the sounds of the ocean

GREAT JOURNEY

Passion flows through my veins

Like the water falls in Zimbabwe

My love is as strong
as the crashing waves of an ocean

Romance is as mellow
as the sun setting over the Egyptian Pyramids

Heart as big as the continent of Africa

I AM ME!

Knowledge to pass onto others
that seek Sankofa

Nurturing my loved ones
as a Mother who loves her child

Thoughts of my future...please me

Those in my life are the pillars in my temple

Holding me up through the good and dismal

Those who hold my hand
feel the strength of a warrior

And the knowledge of an elder

Those who embrace me feel
the warmth of the sun
as it blazes over the Sahara Desert

I AM ME!

Divinity flows through me
as God guides me through my paths

Journey after journey

I seek more knowledge
and see things that I want to see

Learning from different traditions and religions

Pleases me!

My face is young but my tongue is old

For I speak the wisdom
the ancestors have passed onto me

I sit underneath a Baobob tree

Listening to the cool wind as I feel the breeze

Raising my hands high
to give the ancestors praise

On this glorious day I think
of all I've been through

From birth to childhood to adulthood

I am amazed

As I walk to the well
I think about my American ways

How they tried to brainwash my people

To believe that your natural hair is nappy,
your color is too dark and your features

Are just not good enough

HOW DARE THEY!

Coming back HOME taught me a lesson

As I feel the hot sand beneath my feet

Wondering why it took so long
to come back home

I am on a journey, would you care to join me

To free my people's minds and spirits

And let them know that black
is beautiful no matter what shade

And to free your hair and do your thang!

I am on a journey through Africa

A journey to be one with myself

Free my mind and everything about me

LUNAVERSOUL
BY Samax Amen

MUSIC MAKES ME HIGH

Sweet sounds of music takes me
to a hidden paradise within my soul

A place where I can forget
about my problems of yesterday

And dream a dream of today

This place is hidden deep in my soul

A treasure, a pearl, a place where no one knows

Where the beats and rhythms take control

Soft and loud voices singing to my soul

Hidden in the depths of my heart...

Smooth tunes soothing

Comforting

Healing

As I begin

Exhaling

Sweet voices

Singing to me

Musicians

Playing at my heart strings

Beating on the drum of my heart

Conducting

Songs

Leading me to

Everlasting

Healing

Whisking me away

To a place

Deep within my soul

A place where no one knows

But Him

And Me

BLESS THE DJ
BY Riki Johnson-Atkins

GOD'S WHISPER

God spoke to me

In my darkest hour

In a whisper

As I cried for days and nights

I finally heard His voice
My loud sobs turned into whimpers,
something quieting my spirit suddenly

A voice so softly

Gently

At the midnight hour

Told me, "I will get you through

Speak to the mountains in your life my child

Tell them your problems, talk to THEM

Declare to Me that you will get through this and let me
inside

Look out into the dark night my child
and know I will get you over the mountains."

The voice began to speak more loudly as He said,

"SPEAK TO IT"

He thought I wasn't listening
as His voice grew in the dark of night and yelled,

SPEAK TO IT!

As the dawn arose, I awoke to feeling
the Holy Spirit blanket me

A shield of protection
as my heart began to get lighter
I started singing and praising His name

As the sun began to shine
and the clouds cleared in my life

I lifted my hands and shouted, "Thank You!"

It felt so wonderful to shout so I did it again;
I yelled even louder

"Thank You Jesus!"

I spoke to the mountain asking for God
to forgive those that trespassed against me

I spoke to the other mountain
and I asked God to forgive me for I have sinned

Praying for a new day and a lighter soul

At that moment, I forgave my enemies

It was in that moment that I left my past behind

I prayed for my financial burdens to be gone

Those in my life causing chaos
and confusion to fade away

The death of my relationship
that I was still mourning to finally cease
and allow God to comfort me

I now lived for the future and prayed
for those I left on the mountain

Not everyone can walk with you
on your spiritual journey

Not everyone can walk the same path
to the same beat as you

In that waking moment I knew I was FREE!

Free from emotional distress

Free from having my spirit enslaved

Free from mental bondage

Free from feeling alone and desperate

I was FREE!

Speak to me Lord

Thank You

Speak to me God

Thank you God

I AM FREE!

TRUST
BY David Rodriguez

NYAME DUA

"Tree of God" — Altar
Symbol of God's presence and protection
(Willis, The Adinkra Dictionary)

DIVINE MOLD

God will bless me with a chaser

And I don't mean alcohol

I'm talking about a man who believes
in that old fashion love

He'll pursue ME and when he catches me
he will never let go

See, I am a creature of my Father God

Unique and divine in every aspect

Gifted in His eyes

I'm here to school those

Who can't appreciate that lovin'
only your Grandma can talk about

I know that just as I was created
in God's eyes for someone

In return...God has made someone for me

I've quieted my soul and turned off
all negative voices that just don't know

God is my radar screen
when it comes to Him leading me

Instead of trusting in Him in the past,
I trusted myself and lost sight of my way

Finding love in all the wrong places

Led astray from my faith in you God

Forgive me as I give all to you

God I'm going to keep praying

And must believe it's all in your time

In the meantime, I'm going to sit back and wait

For my blessing to appear

Sitting patiently

For that old fashion…old school lovin'

That only You will know

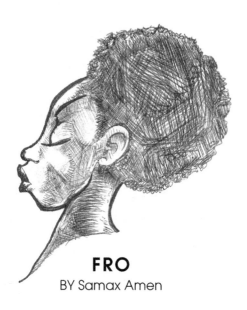

FRO
BY Samax Amen

THE ROOTS

Oooooh chile will you look at this tree

My how much it has grown

From an itty bitty branch

To an overgrown oak

I remember when I picked that tree

Out of a bunch

I sure had a hunch

That itty bitty tree

Would grow oh so much

My goodness, that was only two years ago

She stood tall and strong amongst the others

Even her roots were mature compared to the
rest

Couldn't believe she was so young

I bent down to look at her roots

Hmmm…hmm…hmm

She sure showed me some!

Of what she had been through

Some roots were cracked
and bark was chipped away

From the season before

And even one of her branches hung low

But that tree was strong
I looked closer and

I was overcome

The bark that had chipped away

Was slowly being replaced with new growth

Hmmph and the roots looked nurtured

With moist soil from the rain the night before

It helped the roots to heal

And where the dead leaves had fallen off

Her branches were preparing for the new

I knew I had to take her home
and plant her in my backyard

Where she could grow, flourish and get some sun

I could nurture her roots by watering them

Pruning her hanging leaves
and treating the old bark

Yes indeed!

She would be restored in no time

After the dead weight was lifted from her

That was just two years ago

And look at her grow

I tell her everyday its okay to get bigger

Grow stronger

Grow more leaves

And have some strong roots

Don't forget where you came from

What you have been through

The weather might be rough sometimes

But your strong roots will keep you grounded

And just think…my baby is not even three yet

Hmmph! You sure showed them!

As you protect us from the rain

Give us shade from the sun

And those beautiful leaves fall

For my babies to play in

Oh yes honey…keep growing

Keep going

And don't let nothing stop you!

Just don't forget about those roots

I'm here to repair them when needed

Nurture and even mend

So your branches won't bend

You are forming into such a beautiful

Blossoming

Oak tree

Keep growing honey until you get old

Then pass on what you have learned

To another soul who may need mending

Pass the root, stay strong and continue to grow

" AYA "

Symbol of endurance and resourcefulness also known as fern.
The fern is a hardy plant that can grow in difficult places.
"An individual who wears this symbol suggests that he has endured
many adversities and outlasted much difficulty."
(Willis, The Adinkra Dictionary)

SPIRITUAL ESCAPE

Please take a journey with me

Close your eyes and picture
a place of peace, love and serenity

As you envy the beauty
that Mother Nature has set before you

Open your eyes and look around
and through the light you see
what He has given you

Appreciate your thoughts, gift of sight
and sound

For your body is a temple

Your mind is a place to let your fantasies
and dreams run wild

Your spirit is the force that protects you

Loves you

And should never be broken

Look deep into your soul
and don't be afraid of what you may find

You see, your soul is that buried treasure
that God gave when He blessed you with life

The sweet soul, that blends in and listens
for instruction from your
everlasting eternal spirit

Even the blows we take
from stress, pressure, work and life
can't break it

When you search your soul, breathe in
as you go deeper into yourself

Relaxation takes over
as your soul listens to your spirit
Ever so often you should take a trip
to get to know yourself

Know the presence that He has given

To know the love that is expressed
through our spirits

Please take a journey with me

Be at peace

Take time to give God thanks for this gift of life
and behold your destiny

RISING
BY Riki Johnson-Atkins

Love
Yourself
Before
You
Love
Someone
Else

The journey continues…

Not quite the end

Turn the page…

Now It's Your Turn...

Write,
Draw,
Paint,
Love...

— Peace

CREATIVE PAGES

CREATIVE PAGES

CREATIVE PAGES

CREATIVE PAGES

ABOUT THE AUTHOR

S erena Theresa Wills is a native New Yorker and currently re-
sides in the Washington, DC area. She holds a Bachelor of Arts
Degree in Policy Studies from Syracuse University and a Mas-
ter Degree in Public Administration from Virginia Tech.

During her literary journey Serena moved to Dallas, Texas for
three and half years, where she focused on honing her craft and be-
came published. She completed several manuscripts and children's
stories. Her publication credentials include being a contributing au-
thor in *Gumbo for the Soul, Here's Our Child Where's the Village and
Gumbo for the Soul, Women of Honor—Special Pink Edition* edited
by Beverly Black-Johnson, *Have a Little Faith* and *Keeping the Faith*
edited by Vanessa Miller, and *How I Freed My Soul, Liberated Muse,
Volume 1, Betrayal Wears a Pretty Face, Liberated Muse, Volume
2* edited by Khadijah Ali-Coleman and the most recently published
anthology, *Cornbread, Fish and Collard Greens—Prayers, Poems and
Affirmations for People Living with HIV/AIDS* edited by Khafre Abif.

Serena also has an extensive background in the nonprofit field
concentrating on youth development, literacy and arts education.
Serena uses her writing and spoken word art to provide workshops
to school age children to help them with writing, communication
skills and public speaking.

Serena is a mother to her beautiful son, has worked in the non-profit field for over sixteen years and spends her spare time enjoying family, traveling, running, African dance and serves her community through the sisterhood of Delta Sigma Theta Sorority, Inc.

For more information on her publications and booking, please go to www.serenawills.com

*A*wakening

a book of poetry

Pieces of Life
Volume II

Serena Wills

HEALED WOUNDS

Scars that were deep

Bleeding profusely nonstop

Battle wounds from loving the wrong people

Losing my friends and family tragically

Broken love from a man I once adored

Questioning whether I'm being punished

If I did something wrong to deserve this

Crawling to the rock
where I see people standing strong

I reached out and then it dawned on me

My wounds each told a story

Test became my testimony

The more I extended my arm I began to see

The wounds healing...

REGAINING MOMENTUM

Borderline of life and death

Shining light on my face

Arms extended to me

Loved ones who don't want to see me
in pain or distress

Wanting my body to heal

I hear my daughter's voice that has passed on

Telling me, "Mommy I miss you."

I walk towards her into the light

Then it hit me

My work isn't done here yet

Hands haven't touched all those that God
has set out for me to love

Mind thinking overtime

Which way do I go

Do I walk towards my beloved child
that passed away just three years ago

Or make an about face to my family
that still needs me...

DA FLIP!

This is how I feel

Your life has been flipped upside down

360 degrees

You didn't ask for it, you didn't want it

The confusion that has commenced over night

But it's hear and there is no need
to fuss and fight

It's here and you didn't want it

Your life got flipped upside down

360 degrees

Because she wasn't careful

She wasn't careful

See baby girl was confused

And as her mama sang the blues

And Daddy went to prison

She was in a state of confusion
and needed intervention...

CRYING TEARS
OF TEAL

a poetry book

Serena Wills

CRYING TEARS OF TEAL

Tears glistening against my skin

A sea of water streaming down my face

Uncontrollable as I felt hopeless

God I have to save her...
I love her and don't want to let go

How can she be stricken with cancer...
my mother...the woman I adore

Locked in a room so I wouldn't upset her

Crying tears of teal for ovarian cancer

I went from a daughter to a caregiver

Mommy please don't give up the fight

We can win this battle...right?

Crying together I began to see a wave of teal

Promising each other to go on day by day

Hoping to God that there is a way for her to stay

I cry tears of teal like I suffered a battle wound

Feeling like a yo-yo back and forth trying to find
answers to a diagnosis that I couldn't swallow...

WHIMSICAL MOMENTS

You're my air

Into your eyes I glare

Knowing that I received the ultimate prize

You as a mother

And I as your daughter

Still moments in time
will be remembered forever

From watching you grace the stage with dance

Having deep conversations with me
about forgiving people and sometimes
giving them a second chance

From the night you held me tight
when I heard my father died

Wiping away a steady flow of tears as I cried

Being my warrior through many battles

Dry days to stark nights you were my water...

SURVIVOR

I SURVIVED!

CANCER IS NO LONGER ALIVE

IN MY BLOOD, ORGANS
AND WHOLE BODY!

Now I'm not going to lie

All the while I was sick
with this wretched illness
I knew I would survive

Yeah I was scared

At times I dreamt of my death bed

But when I awoke I knew
I was given another day

One more chance to get better as I lay

In a hospital bed

I was even told hospice might be my only bet

I didn't believe those lies
and instead I fought on and survived!

I SURVIVED!...

ART COLLECTIVES, COMPANIES AND ORGANIZATIONS TO SUPPORT:

Art Conspiracy, Inc: Supporting arts organizations through an annual funky fundraising event that includes a live auction, music and other eclectic activities. Check them out at www.artconspiracy.org

ArtLoveMagic, Inc: A nonprofit that focuses on nurturing and embracing all artists through workshops, live art shows, open mics, programming for youth and much more. Check them out on the web at www.artlovemagic.com

Big Thought: A nonprofit that infuses the arts and creative outlets into youth and families through schools, communities, organizations and city agencies in Dallas, TX. For more information on how to get involved and to bring the arts into your children's world visit them at www.bigthought.org

BloomBars: is turning a concept to unite communities through the arts into a model for energizing and inspiring communities to strive for personal and collective progress. Established in 2008 in Washington, DC's burgeoning Columbia Heights neighborhood, BloomBars is driven by a volunteer team of artists, educators, and community and business leaders. Redefining the perception of a bar, BloomBars doesn't serve or allow alcohol on its premises fostering a safe and family-friendly environment. Please visit them at www.bloombars.org

coup d'etat Brooklyn: Their slogan is exactly how you feel wearing their clothes. Live to change something. All of their tees, sweatshirts and jackets have a meaning from Teach the Babies to Peace, Unity, Love and Havin' Fun! Get a tee and support the cause at www.cdtbk.com

Divine Wryte Creations, LLC: founded by Serena Wills this company offers two distinct services of creativity and consulting. Choose from the creative line to purchase books, framed poetry, gifts with a poetic flare and more. Or inquire about the consulting services for nonprofits, foundations and schools. Services include workshops on strategic planning, board development, partnership development, writing, poetry and more. Visit the website at www.serenawills.com

Guerilla Arts Ink: a community based organization specializing in innovative education, cultural arts programming and professional development. For more information and how to get involved go to http://wethewilling.org or http://edlyrics.com

Gumbo for the Soul: a savory blend of anthologies that focus on humanitarian issues affecting communities worldwide! From education to adoption and everything in between, we will bring inspirational and informative publications that promise to spark change, heighten awareness and offer resources and resolutions to the issues we outline. www.gumboforthesoul.com

Liberated Muse Productions: An arts collective based out of Washington, DC is an online community of artists and patrons putting on various events throughout the year. Check them out at www.liberatedmuse.com

Preservation LINK: This dynamic Dallas based organization offers arts-in-education programs for youth from fourth to twelfth grades. Their focus is audio/visual media which allows youth to develop and share thoughts and feelings about their communities. Children and teens spend time learning how to capture life through the eye of a camera lens and take photographs; critically think about social issues, effective communication strategies, creative writing and how to research the facts to tell the story. For more information go to www.preservationlink.org

Sojournals: A social network and urban media aggregator. Based in Washington, DC one can network with local artists, businesses, and nonprofits to collaborate on projects. It's also a media outlet for what's really happening in DC. http://sojournals.wordpress.com

South Dallas Cultural Center: A multifaceted afro centric multimedia and fine arts center. The Center offers cultural arts enrichment classes with an emphasis on service to youth and adults of South Dallas. For more information on events, classes and workshops go to their website at www.dallasculture.org/sdculturalcenter

SERENE
BY Samax Amen

For more information on events,
book signings and how to book the artist,
please go to www.serenawills.com
or email serena@serenawills.com

Also, please join Serena Wills on Facebook
at www.facebook.com/serenawills
and on Twitter under divinewryte